Breathing

Anita Ganeri

Watts Books
London • New York • Sydney

© 1994 Watts Books

Watts Books
96 Leonard Street
London EC2A 4RH

Franklin Watts Australia
14 Mars Road
Lane Cove
NSW 2066

UK ISBN: 0 7496 1491 9

10 9 8 7 6 5 4 3 2 1

Series editor: Pippa Pollard
Editor: Jane Walker
Design: Sally Boothroyd
Artwork: Helen Parsley
Photo research: Juliet Duff

A CIP catalogue record for this book
is available from the British Library

Dewey Decimal Classification 612.2

Printed in Italy by G. Canale and C. SpA

Contents

Why do we breathe?

We all need to breathe to get air into our bodies. The air we breathe in contains **oxygen**, which keeps us alive. The oxygen travels around our bodies to all our cells. They use it to make energy to keep our bodies going. When we breathe out, we get rid of waste **carbon dioxide** gas.

▽ We breathe in and out about 50 million times in our lifetime.

The breathing machine

Breathing uses many different parts of your body. When you breathe in, air goes through your nose and down your windpipe, or **trachea**. Inside your chest, your windpipe divides into two smaller tubes. They are called bronchi. They lead into your lungs. Then your bronchi branch again and again into smaller and smaller tubes. These are called bronchioles. They have tiny pockets of air on the end, called **alveoli**.

▷ All the body parts used in breathing make up your respiratory system.

▽ Your rib cage protects your delicate lungs and heart from being knocked.

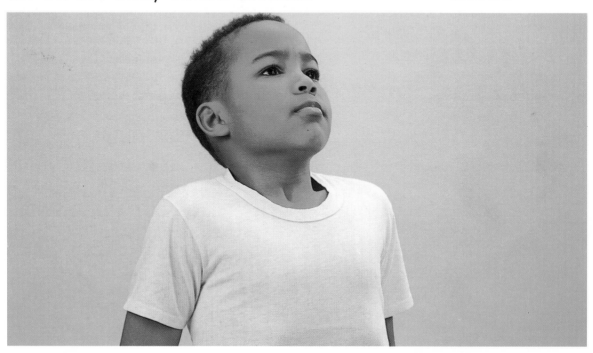

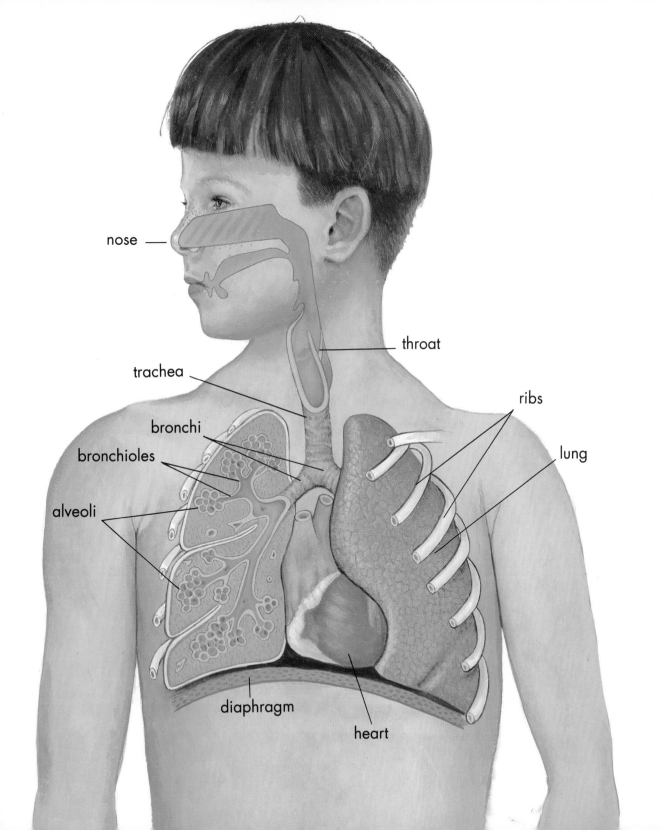

nose

throat

trachea

ribs

bronchi

lung

bronchioles

alveoli

diaphragm

heart

In and out

There is a special flat sheet of muscle inside your chest. It is called the **diaphragm**. When you breathe in, your diaphragm moves down. Your other chest muscles pull your ribs out and up. This causes your lungs to fill up with air. When you breathe out, your ribs and diaphragm press inwards. This squeezes stale air out of your lungs.

▷ When you blow up a balloon, you fill it with the stale air from your lungs.

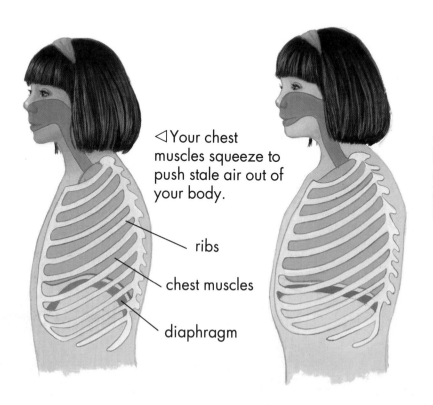

◁ Your chest muscles squeeze to push stale air out of your body.

ribs

chest muscles

diaphragm

◁ When you breathe in, air is sucked in to fill the extra space in your lungs.

Your lungs

Your lungs are like two big spongy bags inside your chest. At the end of the smallest tubes in your lungs are clusters of tiny air bubbles. These are called alveoli. They are surrounded by blood cells. Oxygen from the air you breathe in passes from your lungs into your blood. It is then carried to your cells. Unwanted carbon dioxide passes the other way and is breathed out.

▽ Your left lung is slightly smaller than your right lung, to allow room for your heart.

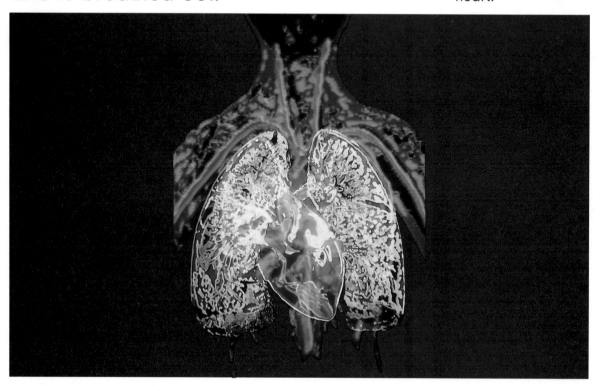

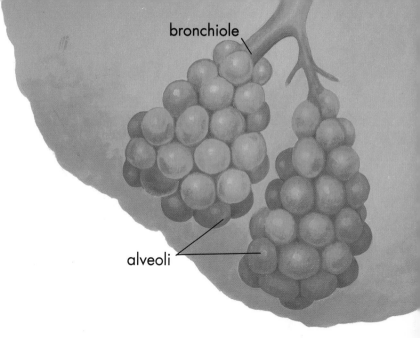

bronchiole

alveoli

▷ There are about 300 million alveoli in each of your lungs. Each alveolus is about the size of a pinhead.

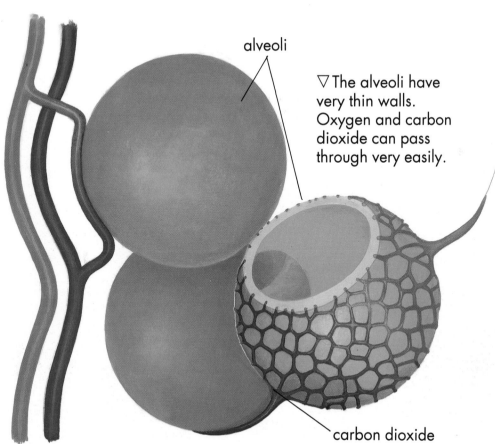

alveoli

▽ The alveoli have very thin walls. Oxygen and carbon dioxide can pass through very easily.

carbon dioxide

Oxygen in the blood

Your blood flows around your body all the time, through tubes called **blood vessels**. It is pumped around by your heart. One of the main jobs of blood is to carry oxygen from your lungs to your cells. It also carries stale blood from your body back to your lungs. Here it gets a fresh supply of oxygen. The oxygen is soaked up by a special chemical in your red blood cells. This chemical is called **haemoglobin**.

▽ Blood looks red if the haemoglobin has soaked up lots of oxygen. It looks purplish-blue if the oxygen is used up.

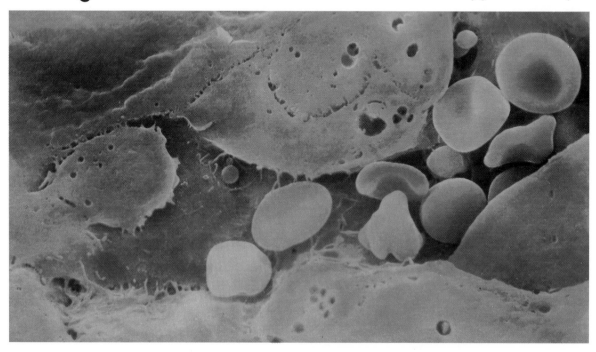

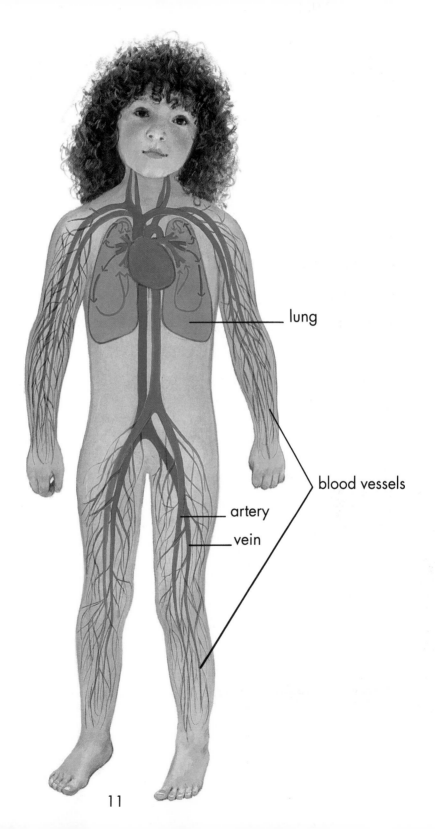

lung

blood vessels

artery

vein

▷ Blood flows
around your body
through blood
vessels. The biggest
vessels are called
arteries and veins.

11

How much air?

You have to breathe all the time. Your cells would die if you stopped breathing. You do not need to think about breathing. If you try to hold your breath for too long, your brain makes you breathe again. The amount of air you breathe depends on what you are doing. If you are resting, you take in about half a cupful of air with each breath. If you are running, you take in up to 6 cupfuls.

▷ Athletes need to breathe deeply to take in extra oxygen for their hard-working muscles.

▽ Your age also affects how many times you breathe every minute. A baby breathes about 40 times a minute. An adult breathes about 15 times a minute. You probably breathe about 30 times a minute.

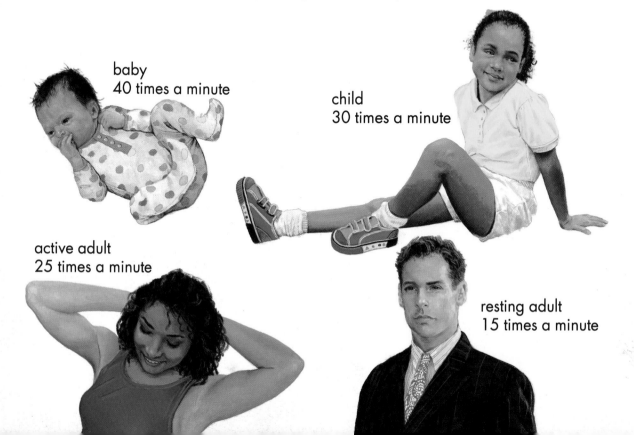

baby
40 times a minute

child
30 times a minute

active adult
25 times a minute

resting adult
15 times a minute

Clean lungs

The air you breathe often contains specks of dust, smoke and dirt. These could block your air tubes and damage your lungs. A slimy liquid called **mucus** lines your nose. Some of the dirt sticks to it. You get rid of it when you blow your nose. Your air tubes are also lined with mucus. They are covered in tiny hairs, called **cilia**. The mucus and cilia trap dirt and push it away from your lungs.

▽ The rows of cilia wave backwards and forwards to push the dirt and mucus away from your lungs.

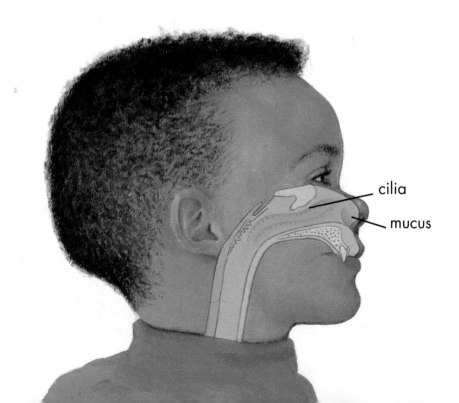

cilia

mucus

▷ When you have a cold, your nose fills up with extra mucus. You need to blow your nose more often to get rid of the mucus.

▽ Factories, cars and power stations add lots of dirt and smoke to the air.

Unhealthy lungs

The cilia in your air tubes are very delicate. They can easily be destroyed. People who smoke cigarettes breathe in poisonous chemicals. These clog up the cilia and stop them working. Mucus and dirt build up in the lungs of smokers. Smoking can cause **fatal** diseases, such as cancer, chronic bronchitis and heart disease.

▷ Your lungs naturally become dirtier as you get older. But a smoker's lungs soon fill up with a sticky black liquid called tar.

▷ Smoking is often banned in public places like cinemas, buses and railway stations. There are many campaigns telling people to stop smoking. It is much better not to start in the first place.

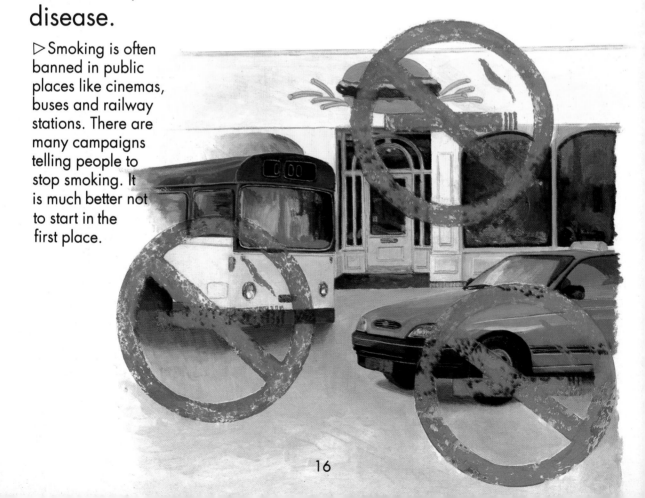

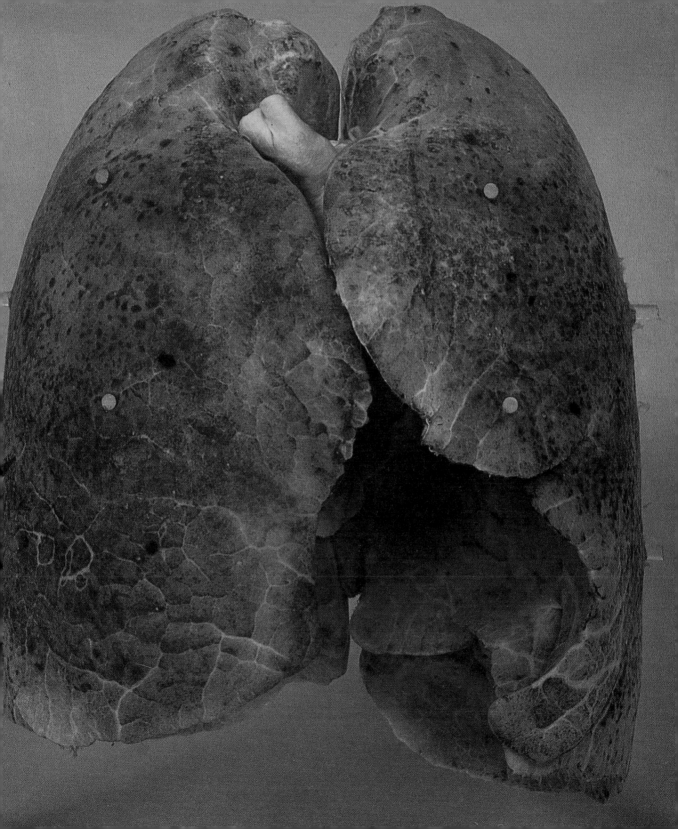

Speaking . . .

You use your **respiratory system** for other things, apart from breathing. Your air tubes are used for making sounds, too. Press on your neck gently. Can you feel a hard lump in your throat? This is your voicebox, or **larynx**. Two stretchy bands lie across it. They are your **vocal cords**. Air flows over your vocal cords, making them shake. This shaking makes sounds.

▷ People speak different languages but they all make sounds in the same way.

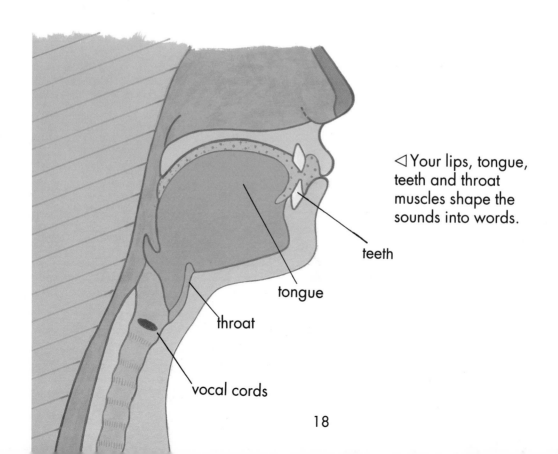

◁ Your lips, tongue, teeth and throat muscles shape the sounds into words.

teeth

tongue

throat

vocal cords

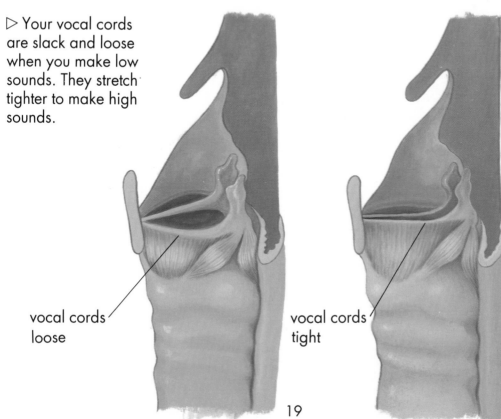

▷ Your vocal cords are slack and loose when you make low sounds. They stretch tighter to make high sounds.

vocal cords loose

vocal cords tight

. . . and singing

You breathe out as you speak or sing. The harder you breathe out, the louder are the sounds you make. The loudness, or volume, of a sound is measured in decibels, or dB for short. Opera singers can sing at about 80 decibels. Sounds above 120 decibels can damage your hearing. When you sing, your ears and your voice work together. Your ears check that you are singing in tune.

▷ Opera singers learn how to control their voices so they do not strain their vocal cords.

▽ Very loud sounds can damage your ears. When a jet aircraft takes off, the volume can measure 140 decibels.

jet aircraft   up to 140 dB

rock band
120 dB

motorcycle
90 dB

pneumatic drill
100 dB

Coughing . . .

You cough to get rid of blockages in your throat or your air tubes. You cannot stop yourself coughing. It is automatic, like breathing. When you cough, you take a sudden breath. Your vocal cords close to shut off your air tubes. Air builds up in your lungs. Then your vocal cords open and the air shoots out of your mouth.

▷ Cough sweets or syrup may help to ease a tickly cough.

▽ You usually breathe out air at a speed of about 8 kilometres per hour. When you cough, air rushes out at 100 kilometres per hour.

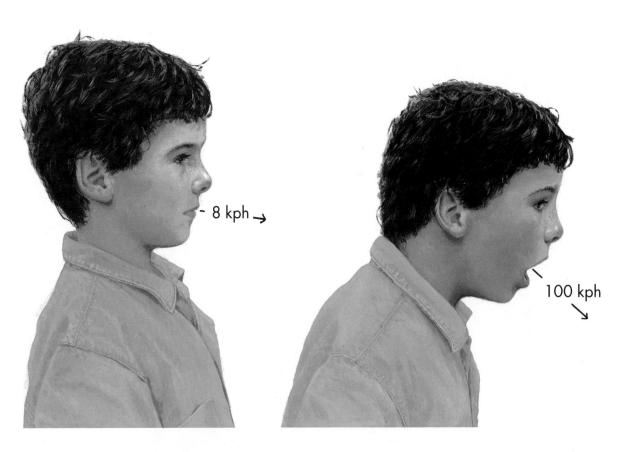

- 8 kph →

100 kph

. . . and sneezing

Like coughing, sneezing is another way of clearing your air tubes. Air builds up in your lungs, then suddenly bursts out of your nose. If you have a cold, you can spread germs when you sneeze or cough. If people breathe in your germs they may catch a cold. Some people sneeze when they are near flower **pollen**, dust or feather pillows.

▷ A sneeze can contain thousands of tiny germs and droplets of mucus.

▷ You may sneeze because you have a cold. Some people sneeze because they are near feathers, dust, pet fur or grass.

24

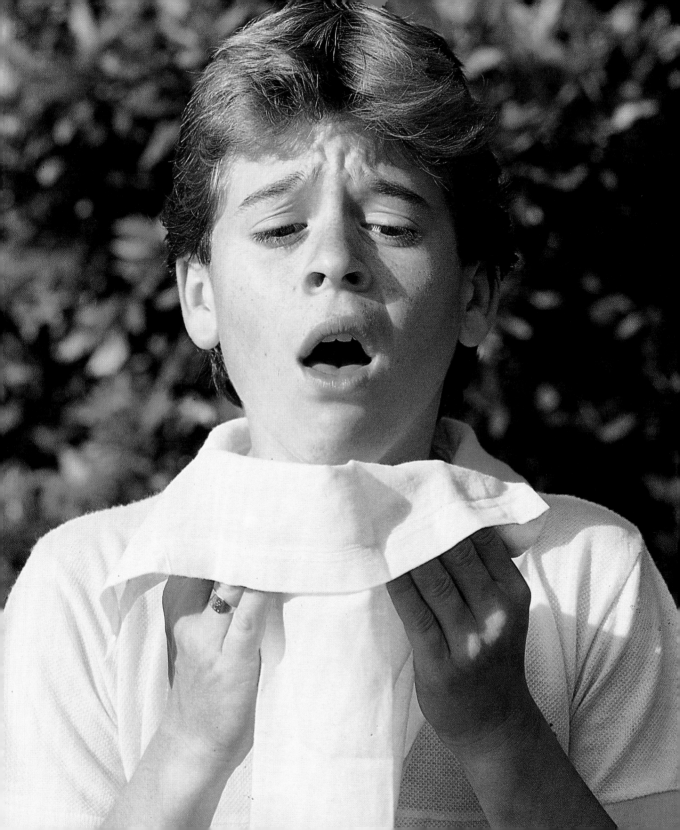

Breathing underwater

Wherever they are, people need to breathe air to stay alive. There is no air underwater. Divers have to hold their breath or take a supply of air with them. Scuba divers breathe air from cylinders on their backs. The air flows along a tube and into a mouthpiece over the diver's mouth. Bubbles appear in the water as the diver breathes out.

▽ Scuba divers can explore beautiful underwater coral reefs.

▷ Air was pumped into this old diving bell through a pipeline that reached about the water's surface.

◁ This fireman needs to enter a building filled with smoke. He has to breathe through a mask.

27

Breathing high up

The higher up you go, the thinner the air becomes. This means that there is less oxygen for you to breathe. Mountain climbers often take extra oxygen supplies to help them breathe. A lack of oxygen can cause an illness, called **altitude sickness**. It makes climbers feel sick, dizzy and out of breath.

▷ The air inside an aircraft cabin is specially controlled so that passengers can breathe easily.

▽ Climbers often need to wear oxygen masks when they are high up on a mountain.

▽ Quechua Indians live in the Andes Mountains in South America. They have bigger hearts and lungs than other people to help them breathe higher up.

Things to do

- Sing a note as you breathe out. While you are breathing hard, the note will sound loud and strong. As you run out of breath, the note will get weak and wobbly.

- Count how many times a minute you breathe while you are sitting quietly. Compare it to your breathing rate after you have been running or walking about.

- Find out more about why smoking is bad for people. You can pick up leaflets about it in your doctor's surgery.

Glossary

altitude sickness An illness caused by the lack of oxygen high up on mountains. It leads to sickness, dizziness and headaches.

alveoli Tiny air bubbles in your lungs. They take in oxygen from the air you breathe, and pass waste carbon dioxide into your lungs to be breathed out.

blood vessel A tiny tube in the whole network of tubes which carry blood around your body.

carbon dioxide A colourless gas which you breathe out as waste.

cilia Tiny hairs inside your air tubes. They keep dirt away from your lungs.

diaphragm The sheet of muscle at the base of your chest.

fatal Something which can kill you.

haemoglobin A special chemical in your blood which soaks up oxygen.

larynx Your voicebox. You can feel it as a lump in your throat.

mucus A slimy, sticky liquid inside your nose and lungs. It traps dirt from the air that you breathe in.

oxygen A colourless gas which you need to breathe in to stay alive.

pollen Yellowish dust-like grains that are made by flowers.

respiratory system The parts of your body which you use for breathing. They include your nose, lungs and diaphragm.

trachea The air tube which runs down your throat to your chest. It is also called your windpipe.

vocal cords Two stretchy bands across your larynx. They wobble to make sounds.

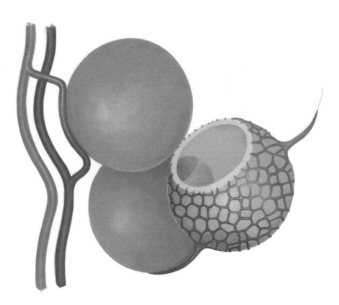

Index

Photographic credits:
J. Allan Cash Ltd 26; Robert Becker/Custom Medical Stock Photo/Science Photo Library 10; Chris Fairclough Colour Library 6, 7, 13; Robert Harding Picture Library 19, 21; Sheila Terry/Science Photo Library 23; John Watney Photo Library 17; ZEFA 3, 8, 15, 25, 29.